The Mouse Bride

STORY BY
Joy Cowley

PAINTINGS BY
David Christiana

SCHOLASTIC INC.
New York Toronto London Auckland Sydney

ISBN 0-590-47504-5

Text copyright © 1995 by Joy Cowley
Illustrations copyright © 1995 by David Christiana.
All rights reserved. Published by Scholastic Inc.

12 11 10 9 8 7 6 5 4 3 2 1   8   7 8 9/9 0 1 2/0

Printed in the U.S.A.   14

For my granddaughter Lucy,
who is small and strong
and beautiful
–J.C.

For my sisters,
Kathy, Lynda, Karen,
and Susan
–D.C.

COME HERE,
and I will tell you a story

about a mouse who hated being a mouse.

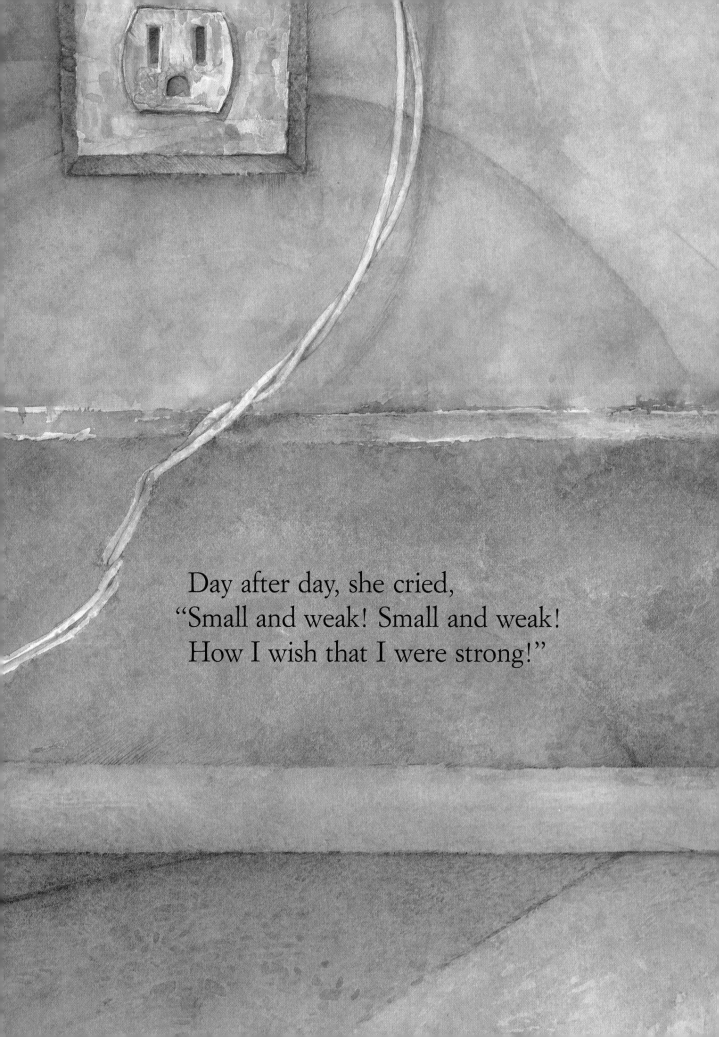

Day after day, she cried,
"Small and weak! Small and weak!
How I wish that I were strong!"

But no amount of crying would change her.
A mouse she was, and a mouse she would stay.

One morning,
she woke up with an idea.
Her whiskers twitched. Her tail flicked.
A light shone in her bright bead eyes.

"I may be small and weak," she said,
"but if I marry someone very strong,
at least I will have strong children."
So the mouse put on her wedding veil.
"I'm going to find the strongest husband
in the world," she said.

The mouse went on a journey,
searching land and sea for a husband.
After many days she came to a mountaintop,
close to the golden sun. She looked up.
Surely there was nothing stronger than the sun.

The mouse called in her loudest squeak,
"Oh, sun, splendid sun!
You are the strongest thing there is.
Please, will you marry me?"

The sun smiled warmly at her.
"You do me a great honor," he said.
"But I am not as strong as you think.

"Do you see that cloud?
He can come across the sky
and completely hide my face.
That cloud is much stronger than I.
Why don't you talk to him?"

The mouse went to the cloud,
who was resting on the mountain.
She called, "Oh, cloud, incredible cloud!
You are the strongest thing there is,
and I want to marry you."

The cloud was a little surprised.
He floated closer and said,
"Dear mouse, you are mistaken.
I am not that strong.
Very soon the wind will come this way.
He will huff a great huff
and blow me clear across the sky.
You should ask the wind to marry you.
He is stronger than I."

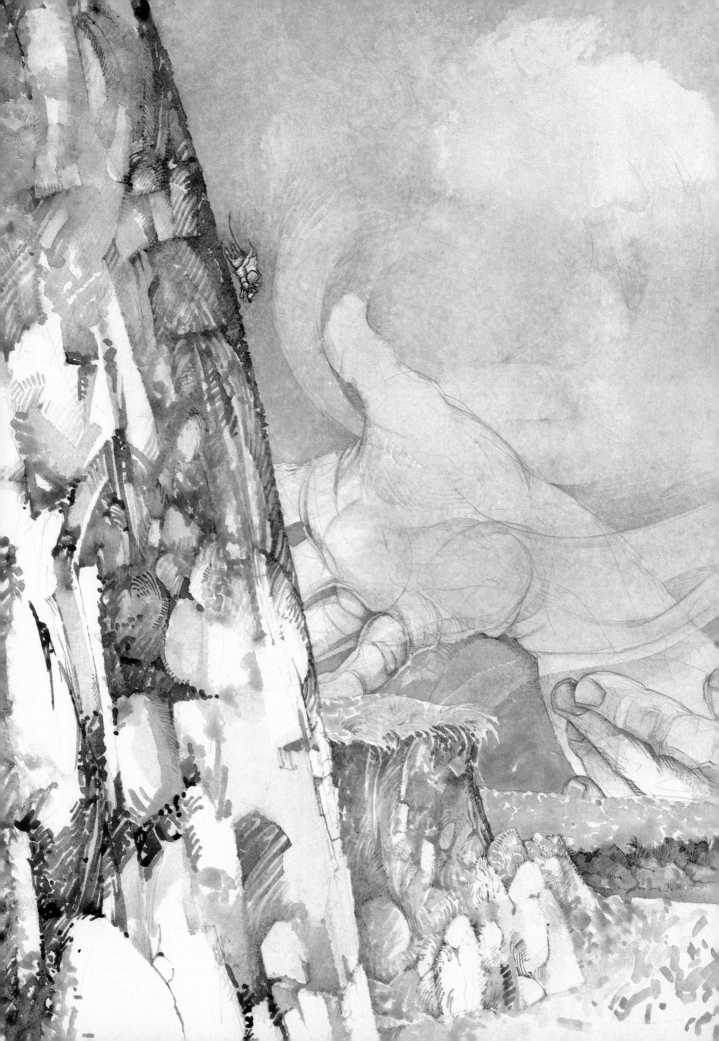

At once the mouse ran down the mountain,
down, down to the sea,
to meet the huffing wind.
"Oh, wind, wonderful wind!
You are the strongest thing there is.
No one is stronger than you.
Please, will you be my husband?"

Gently, the wind ruffled
the mouse's wedding veil.
He whispered in her little ear,
"You gladden my heart and delight my eye.
But there is something I have to tell you.
Beyond this beach there is a farm,
and on the farm there is a tall wooden house.
Day after day, year after year,
I blow against that house,
and it doesn't move an inch.
That house is stronger than I."

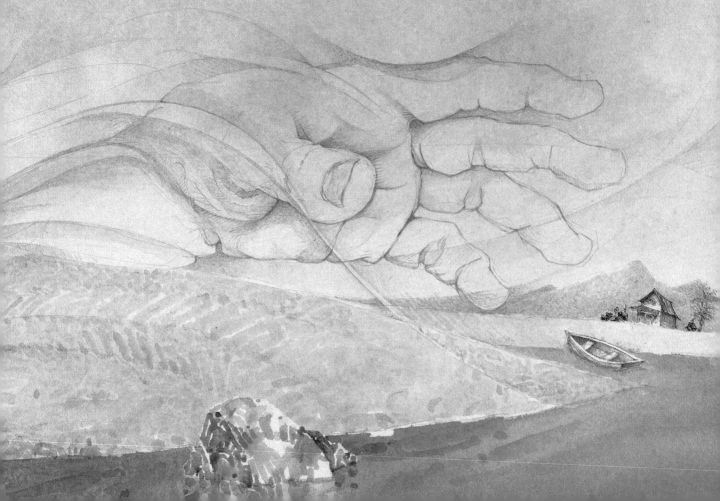

The little mouse ran back up the beach.
She scampered across the farm
and scurried up the path to the house.

"Oh, house, handsome house!"
she cried.
"Please, will you marry me?"

The house
did not
answer her.

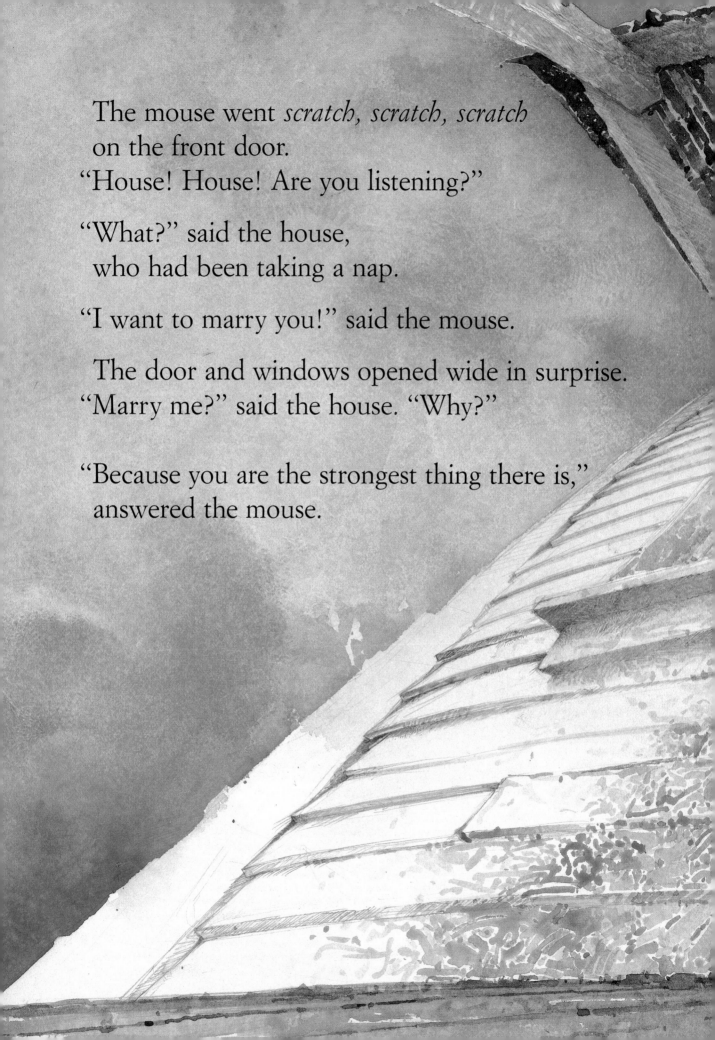

The mouse went *scratch, scratch, scratch*
on the front door.
"House! House! Are you listening?"

"What?" said the house,
who had been taking a nap.

"I want to marry you!" said the mouse.

The door and windows opened wide in surprise.
"Marry me?" said the house. "Why?"

"Because you are the strongest thing there is,"
answered the mouse.

A sigh creaked through the house
from one room to another.
"Oh, no!" he said. "Whoever
told you that is wrong!
Down in my cellar, there is a creature
who nibbles and gnaws at my timbers.

"Day and night he is busy,
nibble and gnaw, nibble and gnaw.
If he keeps on nibbling and gnawing,
I shall collapse in a heap of dust.
That creature is stronger than I.
Ask *him* to marry you."

As quick as a blink,
the mouse ran down to the cellar
and called into the darkness,
"Oh, creature!
Handsome, wonderful, incredible,
splendid creature!
You are stronger than the house,
who is stronger than the wind,
who is stronger than the cloud,
who is stronger than the sun.
You are the strongest thing there is,
and I want to marry you!"

And, yes, you have guessed it:
Out from the depths of the cellar
came another little mouse.